JUST PLANE FUNNY

ROAD WARRIORS UNITE!

DO YOU HAVE A FEAR OF FLYING?
See page 18

ARE YOU A
"ROAD WARRIOR?"
See page 27

JUST
PLANE FUNNY

STEVE KISSELL, CSP
"Certified Speaking Professional"

TIM GARD, CSP
"Certified Speaking Professional"

JUST PLANE FUNNY
ROAD WARRIORS UNITE!

Requests for permission to make copies of any part of the work or information on motivational seminars should be addressed to:

Steve Kissell, CSP
1227 Manchester Ave.
Norfolk, VA 23508
757.423.3867
fax: 757.489.1587
KissellTalks@cs.com
www.kisselltalks.com
1-800-523-4887

Tim Gard, CSP
4150 Ireland Street
Denver, CO 80249
800.865.9939
fax: 303.932.0990
www.TimGard.com
timgard@comicvisions.com

COMPLETED PEOPLE
www.creativevirtualoffice.com
Layout, designed and edited with help from above!

Cover Design By Ad Graphics, Inc.
Cover Illustration by James Malia
Interior Cartoons by Shannon Parish
Special thanks to Don Rinaldo for his humorous cartoon inspirations.

First Edition | © 2001
ISBN 0-9640575-4-9

ACKNOWLEDGMENTS

FROM TIM GARD, CSP

A special thanks to my executive assistant Kirby Campbell Rierson in Montana, who lets me blame her when travel problems occurr (even though it may be my fault), lets me whine about not being upgraded to first class (when she has never flown first class), and who does so well at coordinating how I get from here to there and back again over 100 times a year. I would be remiss if I didn't also thank all the many travel agents I have enjoyed working with over the years, Dixie, Sandy, those nameless travel agents I have fired throughout my traveling career and to my current travel agent Tami, who so far is doing so well. Mostly, thanks to all the airline and hospitality folks who get yelled at (by others, not me) when things go wrong, but rarely get thanked when things are correct. Thank you to all the road warriors who contributed to this book either by act, deed or story, thanks to Shannon Parish, Ad Graphics and all the people who help us to plan our travel and escape from the daily grind.

FROM STEVE KISSELL, CSP

I would like to thank my sister Lynne Priest for her patience and perseverance in helping to put this book together; Alan Klein for his creative ideas; Phil Hines for editing; all the friendly travelers I've met over my years of flying; the cheerful and accommodating flight attendants; especially the ones who allowed me to play on the plane and opened the cabin door when I knocked on the window and showed my ticket! But mostly I would like to thank the luggage handlers for not throwing my bags too far. And I almost forgot ... thanks to the Skycaps who laughed at my collection of 10's and for ensuring my luggage went to the intended destinations!

CONTENTS

J.   JUST PLANE FUNNY STUFF!

FORWARD

*H*ello fellow "Road Warriors" and weekend travelers alike! By purchasing this book you embark upon a new journey with us that we hope will help you to find or discover the 'funny' wherever you may roam!

*T*ogether, Steve and I fly over a quarter million miles each year. As fulltime professional speakers and trainers, we travel both nationally and internationally to provide our services at conferences and meetings.

*W*hen I left the federal government in 1994 and chose to become a "Road Warrior," I never could have imagined the things I would see and experience as I traveled from city to city. I have witnessed fellow travelers at their funniest and most embarrassing moments. All the while, they exhibited bravery and courage, along with cowardice, anger, stupidity and immaturity. I discovered early in my travels that there are two types of airline passengers:

1. Those with a good attitude; AND

2. Those without.

I've noticed that regardless of the amount of air travel experience people have, the division between someone with a good attitude or bad attitude can occur over the smallest problems. At that point, the person will either deal positively with the problem or react negatively and attempt to pass along that behavior to everyone within listening distance. Then, add to the situation the 'extreme' factor.

*A*irline employees deal with extremes every day. They are often cast as the hero or the villain, especially to first time flyers or the other extreme, the frequent flyer. The infrequent flyer often lacks status and status is the magic wand that can bend or break the rules in air travel. I personally have found that status has more meaning with some airlines than with others.

*M*ost frequent-flyer programs have several levels of status. The elite is the 100,000 mile traveler (combined with million-mile status, category of ticket, price of ticket, amount of frequent flyer miles in the bank plus other factors). Status levels are called different things by different airlines and their employees. United calls us "1K" and to Delta we are "Platinum Medallion," however, true airline travelers just say, "Road Warriors."

*F*or some reason as flyers move up the status levels from lowest to highest, they usually "morph" and do one of two things. They either keep a good attitude while they travel, recognizing that airline folks try hard to make their flight a good one, or, they develop a bad attitude and think everyone is out to get them. These people I call the "buttheads." You can tell the buttheads by their cry, "Hey, I'm a 100,000 (IK) mile traveler on this airline each year. You'd think that would mean something around here!" I find the buttheads so amusing when I encounter the 1K buttheads I like to tell them jokes like:

QUESTION: *What is the difference between God and a 1K traveler?*

ANSWER: *God, doesn't think that he is a 1K!*

QUESTION: *Why did they remove the life jackets from under the 1K seats?*

ANSWER: *They don't need them because IKs walk on water!*

Can air travel be stressful? You bet. How you chose to deal with it is a choice.

If you fly, you may encounter severe weather delays, air traffic delays, mechanical problem delays or even lost bags.

During those infrequent times when my luggage has been lost, I've never been able to understand why people yell at the folks in the lost luggage department. They are not responsible for losing the luggage. However, they are the people best able to help you. The last time my luggage was lost, I showed them pictures of me with my arms wrapped around my Briggs and Riley bag with a hand written note which said: *"Wish You Were Here,"* across the top of the photo. They laugh, they talk, they're eager to help. When the lost-baggage agent asks me what my bag looks like, I produce the photo and commented longingly that we've only been together a few days. In every case the agent has laughed and said, "I'll find this one myself."

The key to success is to have fun when we travel,

make the fun available to others, and use fun and laughter to insulate yourself from stressful situations to help you not become a butthead.

The stories in this book are true, or they could have been. And they reflect years and years of travel.

Steve and I hope you enjoy

JUST PLANE FUNNY ...

... *YOU'LL LAUGH YOUR WINGS OFF!*

- *TIM GARD, CSP*

YOU CAN'T MAKE THIS STUFF UP!

CHAPTER ONE

BIG SWEATY GUY (BSG)
by Tim Gard, CSP

I travel a lot. About 150,000 miles each year. I feel that over the years I've become a seasoned road warrior. I've observed that everyone has a favorite place they like to sit on the plane. Some like the window or the aisle, but no one, and I mean no one, wants to sit in the middle seat. And we really don't want the middle seat occupied when we sit down. Over the years, I have observed and perfected many techniques that increase the odds of keeping the middle seat vacant. We put our purses or luggage on the middle seat. Men will lift up the middle seat arm and spread out into the two seats. As people approach we can mentally "will" the person to keep moving. Our mental internal chant or mantra goes something like this. "Keep moving, keep moving, keep moving." The volume of the chant increases proportionately with the size of the person who looks as if they might sit down.

*A*fter the main tide of passengers board, and you think you have adequately defended that middle seat from all takers, they let the standby passengers on. These people are a different breed altogether. They are told emphatically to take any or all remaining empty seats. It's time to break out the big guns. I have on occasion, taken the airsickness bag out and placed it in front of me as if I'm ill. This technique works so well that on a flight from Tampa, a woman looked over at me while I held the bag to my mouth and

asked if I was okay. I explained that I was fine, and that I was just trying to keep others from taking the seat. Next thing I knew, she was taking her airsick bag from the seat pocket and she excitedly asked me, "Can you show me what to do?" We successfully repelled anyone from sitting in the middle seats. Of course the last person you want to sit in the middle seat is the BSG.

All you frequent flyers will know immediately whom I am speaking about when I say the 'Big Sweaty Guy'. I've seen the BSG so many times that I was totally unprepared when it turned out to be me! I was in a small airport and when I arrived, I was pleasantly surprised to discover that my connecting flight was at the gate next to my arrival flight. This gave me about half an hour free before I had to depart. The other connecting passengers literally ran to the connecting flight and I thought, "What rookies they are!" I wandered over to a nearby latté stand and as I visited with the waitress, I noticed that she had '**Pond Scum Candy**' for sale. I teach humor seminars for a living and thought it might be a fun addition to my Comic Visions programs. I quickly purchased all 40 packets.

As I returned to the boarding area, I was surprised to see that everyone was gone. I turned to the gate agent who was just closing the door. I dropped my coffee, grabbed my Pond Scum and ran to the door. The agent said with surprise, "Are you supposed to be on this flight?" I said, "YES, but it's not scheduled to leave for another twenty minutes!" She replied, "There were only three connecting passengers—two got on and they didn't think you were coming." I ran down the jet way only to discover the door to the plane was already closed. The flight attendant was looking at me through the little porthole with an anxious, inquiring look. I frantically made motions to indicate that I was supposed to be on the flight. She suddenly opened the door and said, "Oh great, I have to do the safety instructions again!" I was so surprised, I said, "Bummer." Her next words were, "Please take the next available seat." I was horrified to see that all that was left was one middle seat because my boarding pass said "seat not assigned." Very quietly and as a bead of sweat ran down my face, I realized that I was the designated BSG on that flight. I had even been pre-sweated. I took the only

seat left—between two airport "suits." Both sat reading **USA Today** and totally ignored me. I knew they didn't want me there so I tried extra hard to be a good seat mate and make friends.

They still ignored me.

When we finally pulled out onto the runway, we blew a tire. And after sitting there for a good two hours, I wasn't just the big sweaty guy, I was the big, sweaty *ripe* guy! For the next several hours, I tried everything I could think of to while away the time. I wore down my battery in the lap top computer, read several children's magazines from cover to cover and finally was reduced to studying the safety instructions. Have you ever read them? I was stunned to read on the back of the safety instructions that, **"If you can't read this please contact a flight attendant!"** What did this mean exactly and how could I contact a flight attendant if I couldn't read!

I began to laugh hysterically and tried unsuccessfully to explain my hysterical laughter to the suits next to me. They only raised their papers in front of them to hide behind. With nothing else to do, I tried some of the Pond Scum Candy in my mouth. It's very sour, so I tried to pour a little more in. Suddenly a big clump fell into my mouth. As I continued to read the directions, I noticed the words FOAMING CANDY! *"Wait ten seconds for the foaming affect to take effect."* Horrified, I

"I tried to get up, but my seatbelt was buckled and I just sat there flailing my arms, with this foaming stuff coming out of my mouth."

realized too late that the foaming part started in earnest—not just a little bit, but a lot! I tried to get up, but my seatbelt was on and I just sat there flailing my arms with this foaming stuff coming out of my mouth. The flight attendant tried to help and as she unbuckled my seat, packs of Pond Scum went everywhere. The two suits got up and rapidly left the area while the attendant asked me if I needed an ambulance. Just then the foaming stopped and I was able to bubble out, "I'm okay, it just this candy called Pond Scum, BUT MY SUIT IS RUINED!" She just looked at me and said, "Bummer." Needless to say, the airline suits never came back and as I scanned my space I realized with glee that I was alone and had all three seats to myself!

Now I never travel without a packet of Pond Scum!

DO YOU HAVE A FEAR OF FLYING?
by Tim Gard, CSP

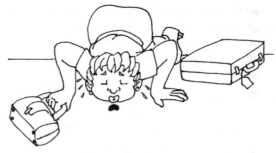

Everyone has an opinion about how safe air travel is (or isn't.) Very few of these opinions are based on scientific fact. If you ever want to know if you should be concerned about how safe or unsafe a flight is, we suggest you visit: **http://www.AmIGoingDown.com**. Go to the site and enter your flight itinerary, and you will receive virtual calculations of the odds that you will (or will not) arrive safely at the airport. The site also offers factual information about airline safety and proves that in terms of accidents per mile, flying is still the safest way to travel. For example, if you flew daily, it would take an average of 1,000 years before the odds favor that you will be involved in a fatal accident.

NEAR MISS
by Steve Kissell, CSP

I am always filled with wonder at the thought of air travel. I am even more dazzled by what occurs to passengers who entrust their lives and worldly possessions to the airlines!

*W*henever I find myself traveling the "friendly skies," I begin to wonder about a few things. You know that little black, indestructible box that is used on planes? Why can't they make the entire plane out of the same material? Why are there flotation devices instead of parachutes under the seats? Why do the flight attendants use phrases like "In the unlikely event of a water landing?" When was the last time you saw a 747 with pontoons under the wings. Or how about this? "For your safety, there are four emergency exits on this aircraft." I'd love to ask, "If we crash and the fuselage breaks open in the middle, is that considered an additional emergency exit?"

*W*hen they ask me if I would like to sit at the rear of the plane, I would like to answer something like, "Sure!" "I really do want to sit all the way in the back. That way I can sail past all the passengers as we hit the ground!"

I especially enjoy the care baggage handlers give to our luggage. When I travel with my boom box, it is in a foam-lined gym bag with red fragile stickers all over it. Hopefully, they won't kick it as far. It amazes me how many extra parts I discover in my gym bag after each flight.

I *really enjoy* flying in small planes. However, I have actually been worried on several occasions because the pilot requested that we relocate ourselves in order to have an equal number of passengers on each side. I couldn't believe it when they requested that the swimmers sit near the exit just in case of an in-water landing. If we really did crash (I mean land in the water), I guess the pilots would instruct the swimmers where land was and graciously thank you to the non-swimmers for flying on their airline!

*B*efore the plane takes off, I sometimes play a few video games at the airport arcade to pass the time. I was shocked once to see a pilot next to me having difficulty with his flight-simulator video game. He became impatient, kicked the machine, and stormed off! After boarding the plane, I happened to glance at the cockpit and there he was! I could only hope that he flew an actual plane better than a simulator.

I couldn't believe my ears when I heard this announcement at an airport: "Would the person who left a hearing aid at Gate 5, please return and pick it up?" DUHHH!! How often have you heard this one? Will the passengers requiring wheelchairs please remain seated?

I understand that in the future airplanes will be nearly fully automated and be issued a visually impaired pilot and a seeing-eye dog for the cockpit. The pilot's job will be to feed the dog. The dog's job will be to bite the pilot if he touches anything.

*N*ot long ago, I flew from Roanoke, Virginia, to my home in Norfolk and there was an Amish family in front of me in the security line. The airport employees were very respectful of them and obviously held them in high regard. All was well until the mother's bag passed through the x-ray. The guard asked the woman if he could examine the contents of her carry-on. Suddenly, all the passengers that were walking by stopped, curious as to the contents of her bag. Not one of those folks had ever seen inside an Amish woman's purse. I never did see what was really in there; maybe something from *Victoria's Secret*. That would have really shaken those folks up.

TIM'S TIMELY TRAVEL TIPS #1
by Tim Gard, CSP

*D*on't use the pillows and blankets of the plane. Did you know the pillows and blankets may not be changed after each flight (do I have to say more?)

BRAIN TEASER:

Two wrongs don't make a right, but can two Wrights make an airplane?

A MOTHER'S WORK IS NEVER DONE
by Steve Kissell, CSP

Another time, I found myself in the bustling city of Aberdeen, South Dakota. I had a plane to catch and four bags to hustle to the front desk and onto the airport shuttle. Overwhelmed, I called the desk and asked if they could send someone up to help me in a few minutes. In preparation, I piled the luggage outside my door and gave my room a final inspection to ensure that I had not left any personal belongings (especially those cute little bottles of shampoo, lotion, soap, shower caps, sewing kits and the extra roll of toilet paper.)

I heard a scuffle outside the door and glanced out to see an elderly woman, much older than my mom (she made me say that), dragging my bags down the hall. "Are you the driver?" She nodded yes as she gasped for breath. "Here, let me help you with those." "Oh, no," she said, breathlessly, "That's my job." I felt so guilty that I held each door open as she passed through the hotel to the front desk and headed for the airport shuttle. When I told a friend of mine the story, he said that I had missed an excellent opportunity to perform for the bystanders in the lobby. He said that I should have held the door open and said to the woman, "Hurry up, Mom. This is the last time that I let you set the alarm clock!"

WARM NUTS AND A MOIST TOWELETTE...
HOW TO NEGOTIATE YOUR WAY DOWN THE ROAD
by John Patrick Dolan, CPAE

My wife Irene and I dreaded flying in coach. We had obtained two frequent flyer program tickets on American Airlines departing from Orange County, California, heading to Dallas, Texas. While riding in coach is not as difficult as traveling in the rowing section of a slave galley...it's close.

What to do? You can never get a first-class upgrade from a frequent flyer mileage ticket...or can you? The counter personnel laughed at my request. The gate personnel rolled their eyes. My last chance was the flight attendant.

Handing my book **Negotiate Like The Pros** to the flight attendant with the inscription, "Thank you for the complimentary first class upgrade you are about to give my wife and me! I held my breath. "Haha!" she said. "Sorry, but you know I can't." "That's okay," I replied; "It never hurts to give it one more try." Then, right before the aircraft left, the flight attendant waved at me and gestured "come forward." First class to Dallas! And they said it couldn't be done!!

The glamour of travel wears thin for many seasoned veterans. Shortcuts, time, and money-savings techniques are a big part of the road warrior's survival.

THANK YOU
FOR THE COMPLIMENTARY FIRST
CLASS UP-GRADE YOU ARE ABOUT
TO GIVE MY WIFE AND ME!

BE AN INFORMED TRAVELER
by Tim Gard, CSP

FREQUENT FLYERS

Frequent-flyer programs can help smooth the way for the frequent traveler. American Airlines, United Airlines, Northwest Air, TWA, Continental and a number of other carriers allow for bonus travel and special benefits for frequent flyers. One or more of these programs is essential to the experienced traveler. Many of the major domestic American carriers are members of world-wide alliances. For example, American Airlines is allied with British Airways, Qantas, Cathay Pacific, Singapore, South African, and others. United and others have similar relationships with major carriers. These programs are free and available to any frequent flyer. Upgrades, other special seating, advanced-boarding privileges and airport-club membership are all negotiable with one of these frequent-flyer programs.

HOTELS

Sheraton International (Starwood), Hilton, Marriott and other major hotel chains have frequent traveler programs, too. Upgrades to suites, concierge or club levels, free nights and travel benefits can all be negotiated with the assistance of these programs. Most importantly, they are many times free of charge to the frequent traveler if you ask.

RESTAURANTS

Tip on the way in. You have a better chance for good service. Ask the maitre'd for his suggestions. In fact, ask them to order your meal. You'll get the chef's best that evening, and you'll make a future friend! But never, never, send your food back. If you do, they will spit in your soup!

WHO SAID THERE ARE NO STUPID QUESTIONS?
by Tim Gard, CSP

On a flight to Kansas City, I was disheartened to discover that I would not be upgraded and would have to board with the others in coach. As I have done hundreds of times, I listened as the gate agent warned us about being limited to two carry-ons, how the flight was to be boarded, yada yada yada.

As she announced first-class boarding, I watched with envy as the passengers walked up the ramp. She then announced frequent-flyer folks and I did the "20 meter mosey" to get in line. As I waited, I heard the attendant say that anyone with young children were also welcome to board at that time. As I stood in line, I watched as a man walked up to the boarding agent and asked, "Do you actually have to have the children with you to board now!?" We all started laughing and he went back to sit down.

✈   ✈   ✈

TRAVELERS BEWARE!
Recently, I traveled to the Dakotas, where a large Asian airline holds its training for flight attendants. One of the gentleman attendants had a few problems with portions of the announcement.
What I remember most vividly was when he ended his speech with,
"We hope you have a nice fright!"
OOPS! I mean flight!

PLEASE SPILL COFFEE ON ME!
by Tim Gard, CSP

On a flight to Singapore, I had been upgraded to first class with my good friend, Scott Friedman. As we sat down, the flight attendant offered us coffee or juice. I chose coffee, and Scott took the juice. The flight attendant immediately warned Scott in a teasing way not to spill the juice. Within seconds, Scott turned in his seat and knocked over my coffee into my lap. My loud gasp of pain brought the flight attendant back to me. She saw my drenched, steaming lap and said, "Go into the bathroom and take off your pants and we'll take care of that." My reply was, "You don't know how long I've waited to have a flight attendant tell me that!"

CARRY ON
by Tim Gard, CSP

I had landed at Denver International Airport and as I stood at the turnstile waiting for my luggage, I was amused to see that several of the folks in the luggage area were wearing pink jackets. I overheard someone say that these folks had been at a Mary Kay cosmetic conference and that they were all very energized! Suddenly, one of the ladies began to shout, "Please let me in. Please let me in!" As the turnstile moved in a circle transporting the luggage around and around, she kept darting in trying to retrieve what I thought was her bag. Directly in front of me she forced her way to the turnstile and reached in and grabbed, of all things, a PEN. She held it up proudly for all to see and her companions let out a loud cheer. I commented, "I think I would have carried that on rather then checking it." Everyone laughed, and she just gave me a dirty look and stalked off. As I waited for my bag, one of the Mary Kay ladies informed me that the woman who had retrieved the pen had been awarded it as a special prize by Mary Kay herself and the "pen lady" had dropped it on the turnstile by mistake.

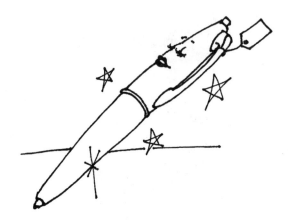

ARE YOU A ROAD WARRIOR?

☐ Do you recognize flight attendants and pilots and know their names? **5 points**

☐ Do you fly more than flight attendants? (*Their* hours are regulated.) **8 points**

☐ Do you know what rule 120.20 is? Rule 240? **10 points**

☐ When you return home does your spouse want to celebrate your return by going out to dinner? **40 points**

☐ Do your friends envy you because you travel so much? **5 points**

☐ Are you able to tell the difference between a 747 and 727at a glance? **10 points**

(Answer at the bottom of this page)

If you answered yes to any of the questions you are a Road Warrior!

TIM'S TIMELY TRAVEL QUESTIONS
by Tim Gard, CSP

*I*f it's so important that we remain seated during the flight, why are flight attendants walking the aisles telling you about it?

? ? ?

*D*id you know that flight attendants do not like to be called stewardesses? And they really hate it when you call them "Beverage Wenches."

? ? ?

*W*hy is it important that we not have our seat reclined during takeoff and landing? After all, if we really do crash, why not be comfortable?

? ? ?

*W*hy do air-traffic controllers refer to planes running into each other on the runway as 'runway incursions'? Don't they know that we are big boys and girls and realize that incursion really means a lot of smoke, fire and a big surprise?

TIM'S TIMELY TRAVEL TIP #2 HOTELS
by Tim Gard, CSP

Always have a routine when going into your room. I do the following: Check to see if the connecting door is locked. Then either unplug or turn off the clock alarm (kids love to set it for a 3 a.m. wake-up call for the next guest). Go into the bathroom, pull the curtain back and check to see if a robber is hiding there. If there is a criminal, you can always defend yourself with your big plastic room key!

AIRLINE TRADITIONS AND FOLKLORE
by Tim Gard, CSP

Over the years there have been stories about airline traditions such as pilots hiding "nudie" pictures in the cockpit for the next pilots to try and find. To this day, some mechanics will tell you they have found pictures hidden in sealed compartments that might have been there for years.

Airline attendants have traditions also. One of the most infamous is putting charcoal around the inside of the oxygen mask that the at- . tendant is using to demonstrate the airbag. This leaves a circle around the attendant's face. They also put notes on the back of attendant's cards which say things like, "Your fly is open" or "You're an idiot" and "No one is listening to you." They've even been known to put naked pictures on the back of the cards of the unsuspecting attendant.

ROAD WARRIORS UNITE!

STORIES FROM OUR READERS AND FRIENDS.
TRUE STORIES – OR THEY COULD BE!

CHAPTER TWO

TIM'S TIMELY TRAVEL TIP #3
by Tim Gard, CSP

I always carry a big alligator clip to hold the hotel curtains together!

INTERNET HUMOR
by Tim Gard, CSP

*W*hen just about everyone had boarded the plane, the flight attendant made a brief announcement. She said, "To the gentleman in seat 18F don't worry about your bag. You'll get it back just as soon as we finish going through it!

*A*s we prepare for takeoff, please make sure your tray tables and seat backs are fully upright in their most uncomfortable position. Once we landed, the attendant told us to remain seated with our seatbelts fastened until we were fully stopped at the gate. Just as we were about to reach the gate, the attendant said, "Don't even think about it!

"*Y*our seat cushions can be used for flotation and in the event of an emergency water landing, please take them with our compliments."

"We do feature a smoking section on this flight. If you must smoke, contact a member of the flight crew and we will escort you to the wing of the airplane."

"We have a man on board who is celebrating his 100th birthday, and this is his first flight! It is also probably his last. So please, when you walk by the cockpit, wish the pilot a happy birthday."

"Smoking in the lavatories is prohibited. Any person caught smoking in the lavatories will be asked to leave the plane immediately."

I was on one of those cramped "commuter" flights recently when the captain announced, "Folks, we have reached our cruising altitude now, so I am going to switch the seat belt sign off. Feel free to wander aimlessly about our spacious cabin."

*P*ilot: "Folks, if you were with us last week, we never got around to mentioning that it was National Procrastination Day. If you get a chance this week, please try to celebrate it. If you can't get to it, then maybe try to do it this weekend, but no big rush. Have a nice day."

TUNED IN AND TURNED ON!

While on a flight home, the man sat listening attentively to the attendant giving the 'safety speech" thing. Because the flight was a "red-eye," she said the cabin light would be dimmed. "If you need additional light, note that pressing the button with the light will turn on your personal overhead light." Then, she said seriously, "Please also be aware that pushing the flight attendant button will NOT turn the flight attendant on!"

SMILEAGE FOR THE DAY:

Trust your Captain but keep your seat belt securely fastened!

TERRIFIC WEBSITE!

GO TO: http://www.funnyscott.com and check out Scott's pick of the best travel websites on the planet. Save a bunch and have fun.

JUST PLANE FUNNY STORIES
FROM TRAVEL AGENTS!

A man called his travel agent, furious about the Florida trip package that was set up for him. The agent asked him what was wrong with his trip to Orlando. He said he was expecting an ocean-view room. The agent tried to explain that it was not possible, since Orlando was in the middle of the state. He replied, "Don't lie to me. I looked on the map, and Florida is a very thin state."

A call came in from a man: "Is it possible to see England from Canada?" He was told no. He then said, "But they look so close on the map."

A man asked an agent how he knew which plane to get on. The agent asked him what he meant. He replied, "I was told my flight number is 823, but none of these darn planes have numbers on them!"

TAKE THE TRAIN OR FLY?

A client called a travel agent to inquire about a travel package to Hawaii. After going over the cost information, the client asked, "Would it be cheaper to fly to California and then take the train to Hawaii?"

PEPSI PLEASE!

A woman called her travel agent and said that she needed to fly to Pepsi Cola on one of the computer planes. I asked her if she meant Pensacola on a commuter plane. The woman replied, "Yes, of course, that's exactly what I meant."

WE COULDN'T MAKE THIS STUFF UP!
by Steve Kissell, CSP

WE LIVE BY THE "CODE" OF TRAVEL

A woman called and asked, "Do airlines put your physical description on your bags so they know whose luggage belongs to who?" The agent said no and then said, "Why do you ask?" She replied, "Well, when I checked in with the airline, they put a tag on my luggage that said FAT, and I'm overweight. Is there any connection?" After putting her on hold for a minute while the agent looked into it

(to laugh hysterically), she came back and explained that the three-digit city code for Fresno is FAT, and the airline was only putting a destination tag on her luggage.

✈ ✈ ✈

I KNEW IT WAS A BIG ANIMAL!

A woman called to make reservations. "I want to go from Chicago to Hippopotamus, New York." The agent was at a loss for words. Finally the agent said, "Are you sure that's the name of the town?" "Yes, what flights do you have?" After some searching the agent came back on the phone and said, "I'm sorry, ma'am. I've looked up every airport code in the country and I can't find a Hippopotamus anywhere." The customer replied, "Oh, don't be silly. Everyone knows where it is. Check your map!" The agent scoured a map of the state of New York and finally said, "You don't mean Buffalo, do you?" "That's it! I knew it was a big animal!"

✈ ✈ ✈

WHO'S CONTROLLING THE AIR TRAFFIC CONTROLLERS?

*T*he Following are actual exchanges between airline pilots and air traffic controllers from around the world.

The controller working a busy pattern told the 727 on down-wind to make a three-sixty (do a complete circle, usually to provide spacing between aircraft). **The pilot** of the 727 complained, *"Do you know it costs us two thousand dollars to make a three-sixty in this plane?"* Without missing a beat, the controller replied, *"Roger, give me the full four thousand dollars worth."*

A DC-10 had an exceedingly long roll out after landing with his approach speed just a little too high.
San Jose Tower: *"American 751, heavy turn right at the end if able. If not, take the Guadeloupe exit from Highway 101 and return to the airport."*

Tower: *"Eastern 702, cleared for takeoff, contact Departure on l24.7."*
Eastern 702*:* *"Tower, Eastern 702 switching to Departure. By the way, as we lifted off, we saw some kind of dead animal at the far end of the runway."*
Tower: *"Continental 635, cleared for takeoff, contact Departure on 124.7, did you copy the report on Eastern?"*
Continental 635: *"Continental 635, cleared for takeoff, and yes, we copied Eastern and we've already notified the caterers."*

JUST PLANE FUNNY STUFF
by Steve Kissell, CSP

*O*n a recent plane trip I was asked to check in at both the curbside and gate area, where I was told to produce an identifying photo. I keep an Elvis driver's license in my wallet for just this sort of occasion. This never fails to get a quick reaction from the employee requesting the I.D. If the Elvis license is deemed not acceptable, I quickly pull out my other official I.D. which has me with a red sticker on my nose. While the official is staring at this picture, I quickly put a real clown nose on! When they look up and see me, they often break out into wonderful laughter...and I often get an upgrade to first class...imagine that!

EXCUSE ME,
COULD YOU REPEAT THAT?

Shortly after landing, while we were still taxiing to the air terminal, a flight attendant made an unusual announcement. He said, "Ladies and Gentlemen, please use caution when opening overhead bins because as you all know, "shift" happens!"

While boarding a very small commuter plane with a friend, I asked the flight attendant what the movie was during the flight. She replied without batting an eye, **"Dumb and Dumber**," as she looked at my traveling companion and me. I quickly replied, "Oh, I thought for sure it was *Honey, I Shrunk the Plane!"*

Visiting extremely large airports has always fascinated me. It is amazing that they can cram so many types of stores in such little spaces. One particular store caught my attention since it was devoted entirely to juggling supplies. At this store, a young woman dressed in brightly colored clothing stood out front juggling all kinds of items in an effort to attract potential customers. I was impressed with her juggling ability and asked her if she could teach me to juggle. She promptly began to instruct me on the basics. She placed a bean bag in my hand and demonstrated how to toss it up in the air. I quickly mastered the single-bag technique. She then placed another bag in my empty hand and showed me how to toss one after the other and to cross them in the air. I quickly caught on, and I could tell that she was impressed. She asked if I was ready for another one, and I told her I wasn't too sure. She gave me a third one and was distracted by a question from a customer. While she wasn't looking, I began what is known as a three ball cascade. It calls for tossing the 3 bean bags high into the air and even doing tricks with them. Oh, did I neglect to tell you that I have been juggling for many years? When she turned around and saw me showing my expertise, she instantly knew that she had been had—she immediately threw the remainder of the bags in her hands at me. "What is that for?" I said innocently. "You're just a great teacher!" I then began to pitch to the passing people, telling them that she had taught me in just three minutes."

On a late night flight from Washington D.C. to Norfolk, VA, I found myself in the company of several sunburned and hung-over college students returning from spring break. Their hair was braided under straw island hats and they all had a faraway look in their eyes. As is often the case when I travel, the plane was delayed because of a "maintenance update." Also, the gate agent was from another country and had a dialect that was difficult to understand. However, since I was a frequent flyer, or rather frequent survivor, I understood the words "maintenance update." The students were having a hard time understanding what was being said, so one of them approached the podium and asked in a slurred voice, "What did you say?" The agent repeated the announcement. The student stared back with a blank look and said, "I can't understand you." I quickly intervened and told the young lad, "She said the plane is broke and in another hour they will tell us if it is fixed!"

*O*n a small commuter flight from Norfolk to Myrtle Beach we were instructed to return all trays to the upright position in preparation for landing. As I did so, the screws fell out of the hinge portion, which prohibited me from properly stowing the tray table. I noticed that the tray was held in place by a rod so I removed it and then the tray came away from its position. I placed the tray in my lap and waited for the attendant to come by. She asked me to please put up the tray, so I handed it to her. Her eyes became wide with surprise and then she raised her voice in my direction and said, "You broke the plane. Come with me!" I knew I was in trouble now! She told me to sit in the back of the plane and not to touch or break anything else. My new seatmates were shocked at what she said and curious at the same time. I glanced at them, and with a shrug of my shoulders remarked defensively, "It wasn't a big piece that I broke."

I recently had a very unusual flight schedule. I was to utilize five different airlines in order to arrive at several cities, all of which I was speaking in. Needless to say, the first four airlines had some type of "mechanical delay," which means in our language that the plane is broken! On the very last leg of this strenuous journey, I found myself booked on a TWA flight. I told the gate agents about how many airlines I had to use on this trip. I asked them if they were expected to depart on time without any delays. The agent looked me straight in the eye and said, "Honey, if this plane has any problems, I am taking you off because it's you that must be causing the problem!"

MARKETING 101
by Steve Kissell, CSP

Recently, I was flying from Norfolk to Seattle and was just passing through the security machine when I noticed a commotion ahead of me just before the end of the conveyor belt. A pilot who was selling candy bars for his kid's school dropped the box on the belt and it burst open. There were chocolate bars everywhere. Soon, there were dollar bills appearing from every direction as people paid for the candy bars and left. The pilot was left only with a wad of money and an empty box. With a wink I passed him and said over my shoulder, "Bet you did that on purpose." He replied with only a wink!

"GOOD NIGHT, BEAUTIFUL!"

By the time the marine pilot arrived at the Naval Air Station, every room at the officer's quarters had been taken. "You've got to have a room somewhere," he pleaded. "Or maybe just a bed, I really don't care where."

"Well, I do have a double room with one occupant, but to tell you the truth, this Navy pilot snores so badly that even people in the next room complain." "No problem," the tired Marine said, "I'll take it."

The next morning the Marine came down for breakfast looking all bright eyed and bushy-tailed. "How'd you sleep?" asked the manager. "Never better," the Marine replied. "No problem with the other guy snoring?" "Nope, I shut him up in no time." said the Marine. "When I went into the room, I went over and gave him a kiss on the cheek and said, "Good night, beautiful," and he sat up all night watching me!"

I'M ON THE FREQUENT-SURVIVOR PLAN MYSELF!
by Steve Kissell, CSP

Ever see the shy guy in the airport holding up a sign with a passenger's name on it?

Greet the sign holder as if you were the person they are waiting for! Chat a bit. Discuss the flight, and then bid them a good day. Can you imagine their surprise when they discover that you were not the person they are waiting for!

The other day I was asked to pick someone up that I did not know at the baggage area at Norfolk International Airport. I created a sign that read, "Your Name Here." He found me right away!

LET ME OUT OF HERE!

A plane was taking off from Kennedy Airport. After it reached a comfortable cruising altitude, the captain made an announcement over the intercom, "Ladies and gentlemen, this is your Captain speaking. Welcome to Flight Number 293, non-stop from New York to Los Angeles. The weather ahead is good and therefore we should have a smooth and uneventful flight. Now sit back and relax. OH, MY GOD!"

*T*here was complete silence in the plane. Moments passed and finally the captain came back on the intercom and said, "Ladies and gentlemen, I am so sorry if I scared you earlier but while I was talking, the attendant brought me a cup of hot coffee and spilled it on my lap. You should see the front of my pants!"

A passenger in coach yelled out, "Yeah, that's nothing, you should see the back of mine!"

PHONE NUMBER FROM ABOVE
by Tim Gard, CSP

After another long day, I again boarded a plane for my flight home. As usual, I took my regular aisle seat. I was happy to discover that the middle seat was empty. This was a good sign. Another good sign was the lady sitting in the window seat reading her book. It looked like it was going to be a quiet ride home for a change.

As we reached our cruising altitude and the in-flight service began, I noticed that the guy in the aisle seat across from me was desperately trying to get the flight attendant's phone number. When the attendant asked if he would like a beverage, he said, "I'd rather buy you one when we land." He introduced himself and stated that he would like to get to know her and told her he owned both a plane and boat—he was using every trick in the book! Through it all, the flight attendant resisted his advances.

The lady in the window seat noticed what was going on, and although I was secretly cheering the guy on, her face and body language showed disdain for the man. She told me that she was a senior flight attendant and was on her way home. I told her that in all my travels and my years and years of flying, I had never been able to get a flight attendant's phone number. She smiled and said, "I'm surprised." I added, "It seems like a rite of passage—I guess I'm not good looking enough." At this point, I did my best to look pitiful.

*S*he smiled again and returned to her book. We flew the rest of the way to Denver. Occasionally, she would get up and stretch her legs. About twenty minutes before we landed in Denver, one of the flight attendants stopped by my seat. She handed me a piece of paper that said, "Hi, I'm Beth. I want to give you my phone number so you can call me when you are in Dallas. You seem like a great guy."

I was a stunned but happy guy! I looked over at the flight attendant sitting by the window seat and she whispered," That's great!" I looked up to see another flight attendant leaning over my shoulder while she gave me a piece of paper. She said, "Excuse me, I'm Anita." "I hope you don't think I'm forward, but here is my phone number. Call me!"

*O*nce again, I looked over at my seatmate in stunned silence. She only smiled and said, "That's amazing!" Within minutes another flight attendant ran by and stopped only long enough to hand me her number and say, "I'm Sally. Call me!"

*S*uddenly, the pilot was on the intercom to announce that we were landing in Denver. By now I was laughing and the flight attendant sitting next to me was smiling. I asked, "What did you do?" At first, she didn't say anything. However, she finally admitted that when she got up to stretch her legs, she made a visit to the main cabin and told the other attendants what I had said. They all agreed to a little plan—which was to inundate me with their numbers. We shared a laugh and then we landed.

I waited until the plane emptied, then exited last. All the flight attendants were packing up. When I walked by, they all were silent until I said, "Thank you, you made my decade!" At this they all burst out laughing. One attendant said they were "hit on" so often that it was nice to turn the tables and "make my day."

*J*ust then, the pilot stuck his head out of the cockpit, saw me and said, "Are you Tim?" "Yes," I said, and he replied, "I don't understand why, but here's my phone number." We all had a great laugh. I walked off the jet-way feeling like a million bucks despite the fact that most of the numbers they gave me started with 555! Since that time, I have made this airline my first choice. I know the flight attendants didn't know me and will probably never realize what their kind gesture did for me during that flight—it meant a great deal to me.

JUST PLANE FUNNY UNPLUGGED!

Flight attendant to passengers: "In the unlikely event that this flight turns into a cruise, your seat cushions can be used as a flotation device."

"Ladies and Gentlemen, as you are all now painfully aware, our Captain has landed in Seattle. From all of us at Airhead Airlines, we'd like to thank you for flying with us today. Please be very careful as you open the overhead bins because you may be killed by falling luggage that shifted during our so-called "touch down.""

After a particularly rough landing during thunderstorms in Memphis, a flight attendant announced, "Please take care when opening the overhead compartments because, after a landing like that, sure as heck everything has shifted!"

From a pilot to his passengers: "We are pleased to have some of the best flight attendants in the industry. Unfortunately, none of them are on this flight."

PLEASE, PLEASE JUST KILL ME!
by Tim Gard, CSP

On a flight to Ontario, Canada, I sat in the aisle seat while a seasoned salesman occupied the window seat. We felt we were blessed not to have a middle seat passenger, and as the cabin door was sealed, we both exchanged a smile and mouthed, "All right." Almost immediately, we heard two little girls behind us laughing, which quickly escalated into squealing, and finally turned into full-blown screaming which seemed to resonate off our skulls as it echoed through our brains. My seatmate did the only thing possible: he gave the famous "Quarter Turn," (turning his head a quarter of the way to translate his displeasure to the girl's parents.)

We watched and listened, expecting the girl's parents to acknowledge his request and to ask the girls to hush. But there was no reaction, and the girls continued to scream even louder. At this point, other passengers were getting restless and looking at the parents to make the girls stop. The salesman once again "voiced" his disapproval, with the accelerated "half-turn!" Again, no reaction.

The salesman became very upset and angrily pushed the flight attendant call button. As it lit up, the salesman pushed it as hard as he could. Now, I thought, we'll see some results. The flight attendant will surely stop this incessant screaming! She smiled, directed her attention to the aisle behind us and said, "What can I get you?" The salesman used his "hitch-hiking" thumb to point towards the back seat where the girls were screaming. While we were wincing, he exclaimed, "Can you stop that?" The flight attendant smiled, redirected her attention to the aisle behind us and said to the parents "Hello, sorry to disturb you, but..." and stopped in mid-sentence. She looked at us with a resigned "there is nothing she could do look" and simply walked away!

Stunned, the salesman and I exchanged looks of disbelief as the screaming began anew. It was time to pull out all the stops and with that, the salesman gave the "full turn." As much as I have flown in the past, I've rarely seen the "full turn" used, and although I agreed that it was past time for its use, a part of me knew that there was going to be big trouble.

Although it lasted only a few seconds, I watched the salesman's face turn from frustration to anger and then confusion. He returned to his full and upright position and muttered two words, "We're screwed." I said to him, "What?" He mumbled back, "We're screwed."

My curiosity overcame my frustration and I looked with the infamous "full turn" behind me. Surprised, I saw two cute little girls playing, and, yes, screaming while their parents spoke to one another in sign language.

Although most parents can be deaf to the noise their kids make, these two parents could not even hear the screams that were threatening to make the salesman's head explode—like a movie I had seen several years ago called, *Scanners.*

The salesman was right: we were in big trouble. Just then the flight attendant appeared, smiled, and said, "I'm sorry, but there is nothing

we can do. However, can I buy you a…" "Yes," he interrupted. "Drink," she continued. "Double scotch," he stated. "How about you sir, can I get you anything? " Yes, vodka please," I said. As I poured my first drink over ice, I looked to my left to see the salesman had already consumed both of his bottles before I could pour mine, and he still had time to push the flight attendant button. The flight attendant appeared and said, "Yes." He abruptly stated, "Two more." Before she could ask, I said, "I'm okay." The flight attendant soon returned with the salesman's drinks.

As the flight attendant walked by, she paused to ask, "Better now?" He responded, "Yes, but we need more scotch," speaking loudly to be heard over the screaming. She replied, "Eight dollars, please." He gave her ten and said, "Keep the change." She responded, "We don't do that." He once again quickly downed two more drinks and then relaxed in his seat.

As we began to land, he once again pushed the call button. Before he could ask, the flight attendant said, "Sorry we are landing. No more scotch." The man began to argue and I hunkered down in my seat and waited for big trouble. There I was, trapped with the salesman, the flight attendant, and the screeching kids.

The flight attendant said more politely, "I'm sorry, no more drinks. Can I do anything else for you?" The screaming continued in the background. I was prepared for certain violence, and waited with baited breath. I looked at the flight attendant, and we both burst out laughing when he replied, "Please, please just kill me!"

TIM'S TIMELY TRAVEL TIPS #4

If your bag is lost and you need necessities. Most airlines will give you an overnight kit and/or give you a voucher to purchase necessities. Always ask for this and remember to thank them.

BED TIME STORY

A father didn't get home until 2:00 a.m. during a bad storm. He found his kids asleep with his wife, scared from the wind and rain. He resigned himself to sleeping in the guest room. However, the next morning he told his kids that it was okay to sleep with Mom during a storm, but not when he was due home. A few weeks later, his wife and kids picked him up at the airport. His son came running into his arms and said loudly so that everyone could hear, "Dad, good news! NO ONE slept with Mommy while you were away THIS TIME!"

LAP CHILD
by Tim Gard, CSP

*I*t was my second flight in three days (a 6:00 p.m. flight home), and as I took my aisle seat for the hundredth time, I nonchalantly and casually scanned my immediate area for any potentially screaming babies, kids who may kick my seat, and beautiful women. (Okay, I'm a guy; it's what we do.) Recon results: status acceptable and no beautiful women in the scanning area. Everything looked okay, except for one potential alert; in the row at my right, I noticed a small child in the middle seat with a woman in the aisle seat—both sound asleep. If you're a frequent traveler, you quickly learn that you can sleep during boarding only if you are totally exhausted, drunk, or both. I decided that neither the child nor woman posed any threat to my solitude. However, there was still that vacant aisle seat next to me. I knew someone could be with them and would occupy the seat, or the child would have been in the window seat protected by the Mom in the middle seat.

*S*uddenly, a small boy about two or three years old, noisily ran down the aisle followed by an exhausted-looking, thirty-something man. The man seemed to be on his last legs, without energy as he walked down the aisle. He had bags under his eyes; his clothes were wrinkled and marked with stains, and the way he walked to his seat reminded me of how condemned prisoners walk as they approach the electric chair.

I had the mental image of Sean Penn in the movie, **Dead Man Walking**. Unlike the father, the child was full of energy. Intuitively, I knew this man was the husband of the sleeping woman to my right, which could only mean that they were my row-mates.

*U*nbelievably, the boy ran past my seat, and I began to thank Saint Christopher, patron saint of travelers. I promised that I would go to church on Sunday to give thanks for the gifts that he had bestowed upon me—if only I was wrong in my assumption and the child really sat twenty rows behind me. I sent my thanks heavenward as I became giddy and excited at what I thought was going to be a glorious reprieve. Alas, it was not to be! My hopes dissolved as a man stopped next to my seat and mumbled, "Come back here" to the child. I saw in his eyes the "thousand-yard stare," a look that I had not witnessed since Viet Nam and the early seventies.

The child ran back to my aisle, and, like a robot, the man slowly turned and glanced wistfully at his wife and small sleeping child. Although I could not see his eyes, I realized the look must have held a combination of love, envy...and possibly hate. As the child ran past us toward the front of the plane, the man heaved a heavy, loud sigh—which sounded like a death rattle. That sigh spoke volumes. He mumbled the boy's name again, and the boy ran back and anxiously waited for the man to sit down. The child excitedly climbed up the man's legs and onto his lap.

Almost immediately, the lap child turned to face his father and began repeatedly to slap him. Each slap was followed by the child's laughter. SMACK! "Ha ha" SMACK! "Ha ha" SMACK! "Ha ha" SMACK! I was fascinated as I watched this out of the corner of my eye. Kind of like when we see an accident on the freeway and slow down to watch. The man sat, looking stoically ahead, while the child continued to pummel him. The father appeared not to notice the whacks from the child; however, passengers in the plane began to stare at this strange scene. The man slowly seemed to come to life from his self-imposed coma. He took the child's hands in his own and said, "Please stop. Would you like me to read to you?" The boy screamed loudly, a primal incoherent scream that reached into my very soul like fingernails on a chalkboard. The boy started acting like he was having a fit. It woke his wife, and she said, "Honey, please!" I watched the man's eyes glaze over once again, and he seemed to resign himself to his

fate; he released the boy's hands and the bizarre ritual began anew with a slap and a laugh. Before the man slowly slipped back into his coma of safety, he turned to me and said, "We have been flying since 6:00 a.m. and I guess it's just easier this way." SLAP! "Ha ha!" SLAP! "Ha ha!"

THE MAGIC WORDS!

*I*n a crowded airline, a five-year-old boy was throwing a temper tantrum. No matter what his frustrated, embarrassed mother did to calm him down, he continued to scream furiously and to kick the seats around him.

*S*uddenly, from the rear of the plane, an elderly minister slowly walked up the aisle. He stopped the flustered mother with an upraised hand. Then the kindly, white-haired, soft-spoken minister leaned down and whispered something into the boy's ear.

*I*nstantly, the boy calmed down, took his mother's hand, and quietly fastened his seat belt.

*A*ll the other passengers burst into spontaneous applause. As the minister slowly made his way back to his seat, one of the flight attendants took him by the sleeve and said, "Excuse me, Reverend, but what magic words did you use on that little boy?"

*T*he old man smiled serenely and said, "I told him if he didn't cut the crap out, I'd kick his frikkin' butt all the way to the moon!"

"WE'RE SORRY, BUT YOUR FLIGHT ..."
by Marylyn B. Schwartz

*F*or those of us who are frequent flyers, we hear those words all too often. Can you relate to this? You're due to catch a departing flight in exactly two and one half hours. Meanwhile you're talking on the phone while simultaneously trying to e-mail a last-minute note to a client, convinced that your clock must have stopped. Three hours have passed since the last time you checked. This can't be possible.

*A*s you throw your clothes into your bag, you hope that they will somehow turn out to be the ones that you want and that they are actually clean. You dump your toiletries on top, grab something to wear other than the tee shirt and sweat pants you have on, and head for the airport, praying all the way that you'll make your flight. As you travel down the highway at warp speed, you change your clothes and put on make-up. I find that a trowel is most effective for this purpose, especially as I age. I just mix a small amount of powdered concrete with a bit of water, some base color and suddenly, I have performed instant plastic surgery!

*Y*ou finally make it to the airport with only twenty minutes to get to the gate. Naturally, the only parking space is in the next state. Undaunted, you get that burst of sprinting energy that only a self-employed person who doesn't get paid if she doesn't make the gig can muster. You make it to the metal detector. You can see the gate

ahead in the distance, and you just know that you can do this.

But NO! It's your turn to have your entire bag inspected by Number 666. You know the one. He's new on the job. His parents were agents for the CIA, but his eyesight was too poor for him to follow in their footsteps. So, angry and vindictive, he does the next best thing—ruins your life. Calmly, you inquire about what he is looking for and you ask him what showed up on the screen. "Nothing in particular, we just can't take any chances today. There seems to be a suspicious looking item, and we need to have a closer look." You then realize that it's a hopeless situation. Dick Tracy is on to your concealed, semi-automatic, handheld umbrella with wind guard. How could you have been so stupid as to think you could get away with it?

You throw your computer bag onto your shoulder, zip up the mangled contents of your suitcase, and breathing hard, run to the gate. You yell out, "Don't close the door, I'm here." The attendant at the counter tries to look sympathetic as she reluctantly points out the departure board. "We're sorry, but your flight is delayed for two hours. We'll inform you of the status as soon as we know anything—which will probably never happen. Why don't you have a seat? You look a bit ill."

GET OUT OF THE WAY, IT'S A STUDENT PILOT!"

G. Gordon Liddy was flying into Miami when all air traffic was diverted to permit a student pilot to land at the airport without having to worry about other planes. When the term "student pilot" is used, pilots immediately understand that they need to fly in a holding pattern to give the new pilot a break.

*T*he TWA pilot picked up on this and used the term when he contacted the tower and said, "This is TWA flight 103 student pilot requesting clearance for landing." He used this term so that he could be next in line to land. When the pilot on the plane informed the passengers what was happening, Liddy remarked, "I always knew TWA used student pilots!"

IT COSTS AN ARM AND LEG TO TRAVEL ANYMORE!

by Steve Kissell, CSP

On a flight from Jacksonville, FL to Norfolk, VA, I was routed through Atlanta. I found myself traveling in an underground rail from Concourse A to B. The automatic doors were not closing and because of the tight schedule, I debated about hopping off and walking to the next concourse. I was just about to step off when I noticed a one-armed man dashing for the doors in front of me.

Suddenly, an announcement was made that the doors were closing; however, the man continued in our direction. Just as he was about to enter the doorway, a thought occurred to me. He certainly wasn't going to keep the doors open with his arm, was he? And just then he did exactly that! The alarms sounded as the door closed on his remaining arm and he fought to re-open the doors by placing this arm further in the door. The doors did open and a secondary alarm sounded. He carefully bounded into a waiting car with the doors closing behind him. I fought to suppress my laughter which erupted into a chuckle while two thoughts popped into my head: Did he lose his arm by doing this before? And, if I had only one remaining arm, would I endanger it by taking unnecessary chances such as this?

GO SOUTH, YOUNG VULTURE...GO SOUTH!
by Steve Kissell, CSP

Did you hear the story about the two vultures who were flying south for the winter? The agent asked them if they wanted to check their baggage and they replied, "No, these are carrion."

PRACTICE SAFE STRESS!

During a particularly stressful time while working on the annual budget, Denise Dakis of United Airlines found a fun way to keep her spirits high. She stuck positive affirmations written on Post-It notes all around her desk, her computer, and her cubicle. Whenever she started feeling low, a funny saying or joke was always within view. The notes were so effective that Denise's coworkers got into the act by placing notes in all the budget coordinator's offices to help lighten their budgetary load.

SPECIAL CUSTOMER SATISFACTION AWARD!

*I*n tribute to those special customers we all love, an award should go to the United Airlines gate agent in Denver for being smart, funny, and making her point with a passenger who probably deserved to fly in the cargo compartment.

A crowded flight was suddenly cancelled, and there was only a single agent rebooking a long line of mad, frustrated travelers. Suddenly, an angry passenger pushed his way to the desk. He slapped his ticket down on the counter and said, "I HAVE to be on this flight, and it has to be FIRST CLASS!" The agent replied, "I'm sorry sir, but I'll be happy to help you just as soon as I finish with these folks!" The passenger was unimpressed. He said out loud so everyone could hear, "Do you have any idea who I am?"

*W*ithout hesitating, the gate agent smiled, grabbed her microphone and said, "May I have your attention please?" She began, "We have a passenger here at the gate WHO DOES NOT KNOW WHO HE IS. If anyone can tell him who he is, would you please come to the gate?" Hey, check your luggage tags!

*E*veryone burst out laughing, which further enraged the man. He glared at the United agent, gritted his teeth, swore, and said, "Screw you." Without flinching, the agent smiled and said, "I'm sorry, sir, but you'll have to stand in line for that, too!"

...SO, WHERE DID YOU SAY YOU GOT YOUR PILOT'S LICENSE?

Overheard on a flight into Amarillo, Texas; during final approach on a particularly windy and bumpy day, the Captain was having a really tough time with the plane. After an extremely hard landing, the flight attendant came on the PA and announced, "Ladies and Gentlemen, welcome to Amarillo. Please remain in your seats with your seat belts fastened while the captain taxis what's left of our airplane to the gate!"

An airline pilot wrote that on a particular flight he had hammered his ship into the runway really hard. The airline had a policy that required the First Officer to stand at the door while the passengers exited, smile, and give them a "Thanks for flying XYZ Airlines." He said that in light of his bad landing, he had a hard time looking passengers in the eye, thinking that some one would have a smart comment. Finally everyone had gotten off except for a little old lady with a cane. She said, Sonny, mind if I ask you a question?" Why, no Ma'am," said the pilot, "What is it?" She calmly asked, " Did we land, or were we shot down?"

"PLAY IT AGAIN, SAM"
by Tim Gard, CSP

I found myself once again at Chicago's O'Hare Airport rushing to get to my gate so I could fly home to Denver. United had just implemented a new size-restrictive template that fits into the opening of the x-ray machines and they now prohibited bags over certain sizes. There were huge lines backed up at the security screening area and it seemed to take forever to get through. People were mad; the security staff were frustrated, and several people were denied entry to their flights. They were asked to return to their respective airlines to check their oversized items which previously they were allowed to carry on. It was the talk of the airport. Some liked the new policy while others hated it. Me, I just wanted to get home.

*W*hen I arrived at my gate, I was disheartened to see that as usual, the flight was going to be very full. The only open seats in the waiting area were next to two men who were playing cello-like instruments, much to the delight of some little girls who stood and watched them play. Intrigued, I went over and sat next to the performers. Eventually, they began to pack the instruments away in specially made large cases in preparation for boarding. I couldn't help but ask them how they had gotten the large carry-on cases through the new security system. They said they had flown in on a smaller commuter flight, but

had heard about the new carry on restrictions. One of the men explained that he had obtained special permission from the gate agent when they arrived at the gate, to carry the instruments on board in spite of the new regulations.

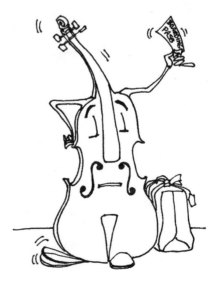

*J*ust then they started boarding the flight, and I heard the gate agent announce, "We are now preboarding for first class and 100,000 flyers." I wasn't in first class, but I was a 1K so I wished the musicians luck and joined the line for early boarding. As I stood in line looking at my boarding pass to see which side of the airplane to head toward, I noticed that my boarding pass did not have the Premier Executive-1K endorsement I always saw on the ticket stub. I knew pre-boarding was only for first class and 1K, so I began to fumble my bag to find my 1K card. Suddenly, a clearly frustrated gate agent repeated the earlier announcement, stating that only first class passengers or 1Ks were allowed to board at this time. Obviously someone had tried to sneak on board early and got caught. I again looked for my 1K card in despiration.

The agent continued her announcement by saying, "Also, anyone with a large instrument, is now welcome to come on board." I thought, "Did I hear her correctly?" One of the guys in line behind me said, "Did she just say what I thought she said?" We both snickered like little schoolboys. Before we could comment further, the gate agent noticed the musicians with the large carrying cases were still not in line. So in a firmer, sterner voice, she said, "I said, anyone with a large instrument is now welcome to board!"

We could hear others in the boarding area laughing out loud, and several people in line were bending over with laughter. I laughed so much that I forgot to look for my 1K card and when the line started to move, I had to give my ticket to the board agent. She noticed that I didn't have my pass marked 1K and said in a steely voice, "Sir, boarding is limited to first class and 1K. Are you a 1K?" Before I could answer, the person behind me said, "Maybe he has a large instrument?" Suddenly, getting the joke, the embarrassed gate agent turned red, ran my ticket and let me on the flight. I never did see the musicians again. Maybe they were in first class!

JUST 'PLANE' FUNNY

AND OTHER

JUST PLANE FUNNY STUFF

CHAPTER THREE

LIGHT FLIGHT – SLIM FAST
Submitted by Dave Compton

I received my private pilot's license in January of 1992. About three months later, I was to attend a family reunion in Butler, Pennsylvania. I live in New Jersey and it would mean a six-hour drive with my parents and two sisters, so I decided instead on a three hour flight in a small plane. I did my usual pre-flight inspection, filled the gas tanks, and got my weather forecast for the trip: ten-knot headwinds for the entire flight. I loaded my clothes, along with some groceries for the long Memorial weekend, and flew off, heading due west.

*B*ecause it was so warm, my watchband began to chafe my wrist, so I took the watch off and laid it on the seat beside me. As I began to climb to my cruising altitude, my watch fell off the seat and out of my reach. Since I was unable to tell what time it was, I had to rely on my charts. Also, the winds were actually blowing at thirty-knots, instead of ten. This caused me to slow down to a third of the groundspeed that I "thought" I was going. I was also using my fuel three times as quickly as I thought. Worried, I watched my fuel indicator move from F" to "E" within a few hours. I got about three miles from the airport, when my propeller stopped and my Piper Cherokee suddenly became a very heavy glider. I followed procedure and lifted my nose up to slow the decent. I spotted a large field, and glided my plane towards it. I made my May-Day call and gave the location.

*A*s I was descending, I suddenly saw some high-tension wires that I was heading towards. I quickly banked a turn. This accomplished two things. The plane flew in the opposite direction, increasing my ground speed and I suddenly experienced a new kind of "Hard Landing." After the plane stopped, I realized that my eyeglasses were gone from my face and that the can of powdered vanilla Slimfast which had been in my bag of groceries had exploded! As I searched for my glasses, the door opened up and a member of the local rescue squad asked, "Are you O.K... Hey, what's all this white powder in here?" I told him to taste it, it really was Slimfast! I sat in the back of the rescue vehicle until we pulled into the driveway to the hospital. Suddenly the medic got worried and said that he would get in trouble if I wasn't on the stretcher—I promptly climbed in back and he strapped me down!

TIM'S TIMELY TRAVEL TIPS #5
by Tim Gard, CSP

I always carry a can of wrinkle free with me. You spray it on your clothing at night and by the next morning your clothing is wrinkle free. It is available in most luggage stores.

I always carry a 12-foot phone cable to connect my phone or the computer because the hotel's line is never long enough.

JUST PLANE UNSIGHTLY HUMOR!

*P*assengers on a small commuter plane are waiting for the flight to leave. They are getting a little impatient, but the airport staff has assured them that the pilots will be there soon, and the flight can take off immediately after that.

*T*he entrance opens, and two men walk up the aisle, dressed in pilots' uniform—both wearing dark glasses, one using a seeing-eye dog and the other tapping his way up the aisle with a cane. Nervous laughter spreads throughout the cabin as the men enter the cockpit. The door closes and the engines start up. The passengers begin glancing around, searching perhaps, for the fact that this is just a joke. However, nothing is forthcoming from the cockpit.

*T*he plane moves faster and faster down the runway, and people at the windows realize that they are headed straight for the water at the edge of the airport territory. As it begins to look as though the plane is about to plunge into the water, and the screams of panicked passengers can be heard throughout the cabin, the plane lifts smoothly into the air. After liftoff, the passengers relax and laugh a little sheepishly. Secure in the knowledge that the plane is in good hands.

*M*eanwhile, in the cockpit, the copilot turns to the pilot and says, "You know, Bob, one of these days, they are going to scream too late, and we're all gonna die."

THE TOURIST PRAYER
Submitted by Lovitt Henderson

Heavenly Father,
look down on us,
your humble, obedient
tourist-servants who travel this earth,
taking photographs, mailing postcards, buying souvenirs,
... and walking around in drip-dry underwear.

We beseech you Lord,
to see that our luggage is not lost
and that our overweight baggage
goes unnoticed at customs.

Give us this day
divine guidance in the selection
of our hotels.
that we may find our reservation honored,
our rooms made up,
and hot water running from the faucets.

Lead us, Dear Lord,
to good inexpensive restaurants
where the food is superb,
the waiter friendly.
Grant us the strength to visit museums,
cathedrals, palaces,
and the castles listed as
"Must see" in the guide books.
And if, perchance
we skip a historic monument to take a nap
after lunch,
have mercy on us,
for our flesh is weak.

FOR HUSBANDS

Dear God,
Keep our wives from shopping
and protect them from bargains they don't need
or can't afford.
Lead them not into temptation,
for they know not what they do.

FOR WIVES

Almighty Father,
Keep our husbands
from leering
at the foreign women and
comparing them to us.
Save them from making fools of themselves
at cafes and nightclubs,
for they know exactly what they do.

FOR EVERYONE

And when our trip is over,
and we return to our loved ones,
grant us the favor of finding someone
who will look
at our home movies
and listen to our stories
so that our lives as tourists
will not have been in vain.

AMEN

TIM'S TIMELY TRAVEL TIPS #6
by Tim Gard, CSP

Never never lose your temper with the agent who is taking your claim. The chances are they were not responsible for the loss of your bag, but they are very important in how quickly you receive your lost bag.

Don't' set yourself up to fail. I always carry what I absolutely need to have for the next day. Most airlines when pushed will tell you they have 48 hours to find your bag before they pay you anything. It's always better to ask" Is there anything else you can help me with?" than to yell at them and demand assistance.

JUST PLANE WITTY WITTICISM
Submitted by Pilots And Flight Attendants

*O*ur flight attendants were trying to help the passengers get settled into their seats for an on-time takeoff. "You are boarded on Flight 1124 bound for Newark, New Jersey," an attendant announced over the public-address system. "If Newark is not in your travel plans today, please speak to a flight attendant right away." The crew helped people stow their carry-ons and urged everyone to be seated; then we heard the plane door shut. "Once again, you are boarded on Flight 1124 bound for Newark," announced the flight attendant. "If Newark was not in your travel plans today, it is now."

CONTRIBUTED BY SUSAN FARRELL

A friend was aboard a plane that landed at sprawling Dallas/Fort Worth Airport. Because of the high volume of air traffic there, it took several minutes for his plane to get to the terminal. As the aircraft continued taxiing, a flight attendant grabbed the microphone. "That's right, folks!" She said. "This is just another way we keep fares low—by driving you halfway there!"

CONTRIBUTED BY DEWITT HENDERSON

*I*n a plane full of people there was a small delay before take off, and everyone was getting a little antsy. Finally, the plane took off. As it leveled off, Brian, who was sitting twenty rows in front of his dad yelled back to him and said, "Hey Dad, do I still have head lice?"

CONTRIBUTED BY SUE KLEINWACHTER:

I SHOULD HAVE WORN BOXERS
Authored by John Hays

*M*y wife and I were flying on United Airlines from Baltimore, MD to Yuma, Arizona via Los Angeles on December 21, 1997, to visit my parents and siblings for the Christmas holiday. We boarded the flight where a center seat awaited me in row sixteen. I am an "aisle guy" because of my 6' 5" frame and 275 pound displacement. My petite wife sat in the window seat and a small Asian woman sat in the aisle seat. "Not bad, I thought." When the doors to the plane closed, the Asian woman offered to move to a seat in the row behind us to give me more room. The long flight was smooth, and I was feeling very comfortable. My wife and I were working on the last of our Christmas cards when suddenly, still an hour from Los Angeles, I suffered a grand mal seizure. It was my first seizure. One moment, I was licking envelopes and the next thing I knew, a man was kneeling in the aisle taking my blood pressure. It seemed like only seconds, but more than a half-hour had passed. My wife told me that I convulsed, stopped breathing, foamed at the mouth, and then went limp. She thought I was dead.

*T*he captain and the doctor discussed the possibility of landing at a closer location, however, we were able to land in Los Angeles. When the paramedics rushed in, they asked if I was able to walk; I quickly realized they were concerned about having to pick me up, all 275 pounds of me! By the expression on their faces, I realized that they were as interested in their backs as they were in my condition.

*T*he captain instructed the first fifteen rows to leave as quickly and quietly as possible. I finally managed to walk with some assistance and fell into a wheel chair. When I arrived at the waiting area, paramedics began plugging wires onto me while bystanders stood by watching the drama unfold. Feeling that I was on display, I didn't think it could get much worse. Boy was I wrong!

*T*he paramedics took me down the jet way where the ambulance was waiting. The steps were steep and I needed some assistance. One of the paramedics was female; she was blond, tanned and toned. She grabbed at my belt and tried to lift me up to take some of the weight off my feet and to help control my descent. Unfortunately, she also grabbed the waistband of my briefs at the same time. As the wedgie developed, I tried to walk a little lighter by using my arms on the handrail. Not knowing what was happening, the attractive paramedic responded by trying to hold me up. I'd lift up, then she would lift. I'd lift. She'd lift. Before long, I had an Olympic-size wedgie. Once I was in the ambulance, I was instructed to lie still and not speak. Only, I wasn't able to speak coherently—not because of the seizure but because of the giant-sized wedgie! My muscles were very sore and I couldn't move because of the IVs. As I lay there, I tried to think of a subtle way to let the doctors or nurses know about my problem. All I could think of were ways to relieve my wedgie.

Finally, at the emergency room of the Daniel Freeman Marina Hospital, I used the restroom to remove my problem before the doctors tended to my seizure worries. I could only fantasize what might have happened when I arrived and they diagnosed my real need. "Doctor Smith, you have a wedgie extraction in room 4. Please bring a winch."

I told this story to the CAT technician who was scanning my head. He couldn't keep from laughing. Hours later, still thinking about my story, he stopped by to see how I was doing. The technician and I continued to chuckle about my experience, even when we left the hospital and went to a hotel that night while I rested before resuming our journey. We had only the clothes on our back since our suitcases continued on to Yuma. After arriving at my parent's home the next day, we all had a good laugh about the wedgie story. To this day, those are the only briefs that I have ever owned, and I have vowed never, never to wear them on an airplane again. I still get a chuckle when I take them out of the drawer, and remind myself that I should have worn boxers!

STOP KICKING THAT MAN'S SEAT!
by Jay Arthur

I was sitting in the aisle seat in the middle of a DC-10 bound for Denver out of New Jersey. A cute, little girl about six years old with long, curly, golden hair was sitting next to me. Her mother sat next to her. No sooner had the plane taken off than the little girl started kicking the seat in front of her. I could feel the vibrations in our row as the small foot reached out to smack the back of 17E directly in front of her. The "suit" she was kicking turned around and frowned.

Noticing the man's distress, the little girl's mother said, "Stop kicking that man's seat." However, the little girl just became more vigorous in her assault on the seat back and table tray. With my background in NLP, Neuro-Linguistic Programming, I knew a little about mis-matchers—people who have to do the opposite of whatever you say. So I said to her, "Don't stop kicking that man's chair..." and her little leg swung to a stop. She looked at her leg and then at me and then back to her leg. She studied her leg as one would a dissected frog in biology class. She knew she'd been had, but didn't know how, so she began to kick the seat again. Once again I said, "Don't stop kicking that man's chair," and once again her leg stopped swinging. By now, her mother had noticed that the strange, bearded-man had twice been able to control the little girl with a short verbal command—and she looked completely perplexed.

After a few moments of contemplation, the little girl must have decided I was worth further notice because she looked up at me and said, "What's your name?" I said, "Jay." She said, "No it's not." (I love mis-matchers!) So I said, mismatching her, "You're right, it's not." She said, "Yes it is." "No, it's not," I replied. "Yes, it is!" she said. "Your name is Jay." "No it's not," I said. "Yes it is! Say it! You're name is Jay!" She demanded that I admit my name was indeed Jay. I replied, "Whatever you say," which seemed to quiet her. Her mother kept eyeing me suspiciously, probably because her once-rowdy daughter was polite and well mannered during the remainder of the flight.

TIM'S TIMELY TRAVEL TIPS # 7

Tip SkyCaps well! $1.00 per bag is the norm, but I always tip more. I don't know if it helps, but when I started doing this, my incidents of lost bags reduced significantly. If I have more than two bags or if one of my bags is very heavy, I tip well when I check them with a skycap.

EXCUSE ME!
Authored by Father Leo Booth

Father Leo Booth, originally from England, had just given up his Episcopal parish in California to speak worldwide and focus on writing books. He was very excited about an opportunity to go to Bali to meet with several renowned authors. After much anticipation, planning, and with great excitement, he arrived at the airport. However, he found out that airline officials were not going to let him fly since he didn't have enough time left on his passport to go all the way to Bali. His only alternative was to fly to England to get his passport renewed. Unfortunately, this would mean missing his date with the other speakers.

After feeling totally frustrated and disappointed, Father Leo quietly decided to put it in God's hands. Surely God wouldn't let him miss an opportunity of a lifetime. Finally, after much conversation, he was allowed to take the plane to Singapore. He felt truly blessed as he entered the plane to continue his flight with the two world-renowned speakers.

In flight, he was fervently saying his prayers when he realized that he needed to use the restroom. He had noticed that a woman had gone in before him, so he waited patiently for her to come out. When she left the bathroom, he noticed that she had her dress tucked into her panty hose, which was exposing much of her backside. Father Leo didn't know what to do. He quickly gave up on the notion of just trying to pull at it without her noticing he finally said, "Excuse me, Madam, you have your dress tucked in your hose."

She paused in mid-stride and without turning, pulled the dress down and said, "I hate it when I do that." She turned and, more than slightly embarrassed, thanked Father Leo Booth for his kindness. She asked where he was headed, and he told her he hoped to go to Bali, but was only sure he would get as far a Singapore. He asked her where she was from. She said that she was English but that she lived in Singapore. Father Leo felt a little shiver go down his spine, and something made him ask what she did for a living. She explained that she worked for the English passport office in Singapore, and the rest is history. By letting her know about her "little problem" when she left the bathroom, Father Leo made a friend and was able to make his connection to Bali.

THE FREQUENT LANDER
Authored by Bill Pfaff

I used to fly a lot. After a dozen or so flights from Denver to Houston, I was considered a "Frequent Flyer." Those of us who have earned that title quickly forget that many of the passengers on any flight are first-time or infrequent flyers.

*O*ne flight went along routinely until we attempted to land in Denver. Fog and winds were terrible, so much so that we were asked to put up our tray tables and use our seat belts. We tried to land, but at the last minute the pilot aborted the landing and quickly regained a holding-pattern altitude. The pilot apologized and explained that the wind at the airport was severe and we would loop around and try again. To my amusement this occurred four more times. Each time we started to land, I would put my book away, and each time we aborted, I would take out my book and begin to read again. This had happened to me many times in the past.

*A*s we approached for our fifth attempt, the plane was rocked by rough air. We veered from side-to-side as the engines labored to compensate. We struck the runway with a mighty thump and double bounced with a deafening noise as the pilot applied the brakes.

*W*hen we finally stopped people broke out in a wild applause. As we exited the plane, an elderly lady seated behind me, exclaimed loudly, "That was rough." As a true frequent flyer, I turned to offer her my sage wisdom when I said, "Planes were made to take it."

*H*er response brought me soundly back to reality when she said, "Well, they may be made to take it but I'm not!"

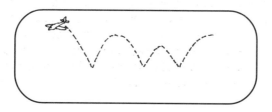

EXCERPTS FROM A VISIT TO PLANET MIRTH!
by Polly Schaack

*H*umorist Polly Schaack is convinced that we should be able to find humor in almost anything that we do—including work. She talks about a flight she was on recently in which the opening remark by the flight attendant ran something like this. "Ladies and Gentleman, there are fifty ways to leave your lover, but only five ways to leave this plane!" And when they approached the airport and were unable to land, the attendant announced, "Our pilot felt so good about his landing, he wanted to do it again!" Also, before they left the plane, the pilot came on and said, "Ladies and Gentlemen, I hope that you enjoyed flying on Pacific Air Flight 87. If not, thank you for flying Delta flight 190!"

*A*nd finally, at the end of the flight, the pilot was seen putting a "for sale" sign in the cockpit window!

*J*ust as the crew did on this flight, Polly suggests that we all go out and try to spread a little cheer. Try it. It really does work!

I'LL TAKE MINE WITH THE SYRUP ON THE SIDE!

THE FOLLOWING IS AN ACTUAL LETTER RECEIVED BY THE PRESIDENT OF ONE OF THE MAJOR AIRLINES—NAMES ARE WITHHELD TO PROTECT THE INNO-CENT OR GUILTY.

Dear Sir,

I would like to report a potential hazard to your passengers by relating my own experience on one of your flights. It was the morning flight from Seattle to Boise, Idaho, with a stop in Portland.

Breakfast was served on the Portland/Boise leg. The breakfast was a fruit cup, a small waffle, and two slices of ham, whipped butter, and pure maple syrup. I love pure maple syrup, and I was very pleased to note that the sealed paper cup in which it was contained was hot.

I set the cup on the tray and lifted the tab. A bronze colored bullet, like a missile, came shooting out of the cup, and without losing a drop on the way, most of that maple syrup hit me on the necktie. It then ran down over my shirt, your seat belt, and my crotch.

The attendant brought me some wet and dry napkins for my shirt and tie, but I couldn't quite bring myself to cleaning my lower part on a crowded plane.

At that time the table did cover things, and what was below was known only to me. One the other hand, what do you do with a syrup-covered crotch on a loaded airplane at 9:10 a.m. on a sunny morning?

Well, I decided to try and go unnoticed to the men's room at the Boise Airport. Getting off the plane was not too bad. I stayed close to the lady ahead of me, and it was okay except for a brief moment when a dangling sleeve of her sweater got stuck on me.

The Boise Airport buildings were completely changed since my last visit, and I had a little trouble finding the men's room. I was pleased to find the airport air conditioned, and the flight wasn't too bad.

The men's room was loaded with the same (but segregated) group that was on my flight. Your stewardesses had been great with the coffee. I finally got a basin, and soaked my handkerchief in the water. I saturated it. It was dripping.

Unfortunately, when I tried to get into the stalls, all the toilets said, "Occupied!"

I suddenly realized that this was going to cost ten cents, so I reached my dry hand in my pocket. Nothing. The wet hand had to go into its pocket. There were two small coins which I brought into view. They were both pennies.

I now had two pennies, two wet hands, a wet handkerchief, and a syrup-soaked crotch in the busy men's room at the Boise Airport! But I didn't let it get to me! I outmaneuvered a forest ranger for position #1 at the free toilet at the end of the line. When he saw me, he just backed off.

It seemed like a long time, but the fellow in the free stall finally came out. I'll say one thing for the Boise Airport. This toilet had a lock on the door. I thank them for that.

I'm not going to tell you how I got rid of all that maple syrup, but I looked worse then when I started. A business associate picked me up at the baggage claim, and he didn't say much except to ask me if the seat belt signs were on for the entire flight?

I any case, I would like to suggest that you quit heating your #@*!#@!* maple syrup.

Sincerely,

P.S. THE PRESIDENT OF THIS AIRLINES SENT THE PASSENGER A GALLON OF PURE MAPLE SYRUP AS A GOODWILL GESTURE.

JUST A LITTLE MORE PLANE FUNNY STUFF BEFORE OUR FINAL LANDING....

FOOD FOR THOUGHT!

When I asked the flight attendant what we were having for dinner, she replied, "It's either feather or leather."

WHERE'D YOU LEARN TO PARK?

And then there was this announcement made by a flight attendant: "Would the passenger in the isle please be seated as the pilot cannot see to backup?"

YOU'RE NOT IN A TIME ZONE, YOU'RE IN THE OZONE!

A nice lady called a travel agent and wanted to know how it was possible that her flight from Detroit left at 8:20 a.m. and she got into Chicago at 8:33 a.m.

I tried to explain that Michigan was an hour ahead of Illinois, but she could not understand the concept of time zones. Finally, I told her the plane went very fast. She actually believed that!

FIELD OF SCREAMS!

Not too long ago, I was on a commuter plane that was small, okay, how small was it?

It was so small that we had to dust a few fields on the way to our destination!

ABOUT THE AUTHORS

STEVE KISSELL, CSP

From a very early age, Steve Kissell, CSP found the need to entertain and amuse people. Even as a child, he loved to see people laugh and enjoy themselves—even at his expense! After joining the Navy, Steve harnessed his enormous drive, enthusiasm, and love of comedy into a variety of children's characters and soon built up a loyal following who enjoyed his performances and shows.

Never one to sit still for long, Steve embarked on a teaching career after leaving the Navy. He molded unsuspecting kindergarten and first graders into his own image——a very scary thought!

Steve says that the path to becoming a humorist and speaker seemed a natural progression after years of perfecting his craft as an entertainer. Early in his speaking career, Steve read about and observed the deepening concern doctors and health officials had about the link between stress and illness.

Conducting his own unofficial surveys and research, he found data to support his beliefs that stress can cause illnesses, both emotional and physical. He also found that companies and corporations were realizing that stressed-out employees can be counterproductive, while an employee who is relatively stress-free has fewer illnesses and a better work record.

Armed with this relatively new information, Steve decided the time was right to take his message to a brand- new audience.

He has spoken both nationally and internationally, and feels fortunate that so far only two states have asked him to leave!

ABOUT STEVE'S PROGRAMS...

As a humorist, author, and motivational speaker, Steve has presented to over 1,000 audiences.

SURVIVING LIFE WITH LAUGHTER *(45 MINUTES TO HALF-DAY)*
This keynote presentation will have participants learning the latest methods to reduce stress-related illnesses and improve employee morale. Explore the positive changes you can make in your approach to work and personal challenges.

TEAM BUILDING WITH HUMOR *(TWO HOURS TO ONE DAY)*
Team Building will assist your organization in bringing together the strengths and talents of your team to meet the challenges of staff reduction, and other stress related factors facing today's workers. This presentation will empower team members to reduce conflict, establish networking, bring about synergy, and change the workplace into a fun place.

PUBLIC SPEAKING 101 *(THREE HOURS TO ONE DAY)*
Steve shares the inside tips from his professional speaking experience. After more than 1,000 presentations, he is able to help organizations get the most from the staff's experiences. Discover how important humor is to any presentation and when to use it.

LEADERSHIP IN A CHANGING ENVIRONMENT *(TWO - THREE HOURS)*
In the face of today's rapidly changing world, the need for quality leadership exists in all sectors of the workplace. As a motivational humorist, philosopher, and author, Steve offers thought-provoking, innovative solutions on creating an environment of success and harmony.

DYNAMIC CUSTOMER SERVICE *(TWO - THREE HOURS)*
An innovative and thought-provoking program, participants will learn the necessary skills to deal with customers in a positive, creative and constructive manner while maintaining employee morale. Participate in fun audience participation activities that will help reduce stress and increase job performance.

ABOUT STEVE'S BOOKS...

SURVIVING LIFE WITH LAUGHTER
Steve's first book tells how to reduce stress in your personal and professional life with some hilarious techniques and stories. You'll want to go to work, just to try them out!

NEVER TAKE COMEDY FROM A STRANGER
Meet Steve's family and friends in his second book. Read as he tells tales about them and his own early years. Find out about the humorous side of chocolate.

HUMOR BY THE DOZEN
Eleven of Steve's professional funny friends each contributed a chapter to bring you a cornucopia of stories. Twelve terrific chapters, each with a different style of humor.

TO ORDER THESE BOOKS OR TO INQUIRE
ABOUT HAVING STEVE PRESENT A PROGRAM CALL:

Mirthworks, Inc.
at 757.423.3867
or write him at
1227 Manchester Avenue
Norfolk, VA 23508
1-800-523-4887

TIM GARD, CSP

TIM GARD, CSP—*T*alented—*I*nnovative—*M*emorable. Tim is fall-out-of-your seat, tears-in-your-eyes, and laugh-out-loud funny. But he is not a stand-up comedian. He is a gifted presenter who uses brilliant timing to weave memorable stories and playful moments into his outrageous presentations. Every fast-paced, interactive Comic Visions program gets people rolling in the aisles as they take away strategies to harness laughter. As a result, they learn to see the world through their own comic vision.

*T*im's extraordinary props make him one of the most popular and original humorists on the platform today. His props are fun and funny but, more importantly, they serve as visual reminders to act — not react — to life's inconveniences.

*F*rom Singapore to Sioux City, Tim has been "cracking 'em up" as a professional speaker since 1984.

REMEMBER, LAUGHTER BECOMES YOU....TIM GARD, CSP

ABOUT TIM'S PROGRAMS AND TIM'S TOY'S

SEMINARS – WORKSHOPS – TEAM DEVELOPMENT

Every fast-paced interactive Comic Visions program is filled with memorable stories, playful moments, and brilliant timing. While you roll in the aisles, Tim subtly slips in strategies of how to use just the right Comic Vision humor option at just the right moment. Attend just one of his programs and you will leave feeling renewed and re-energized, equipped with tangible humor skills you can use immediately— on the job and off.

Once you get people laughing, they're listening and you can tell them almost everything." Herbert Gardner

DEVELOPING A COMIC VISION Keynote (45 minutes to full day)

In this laugh-a-minute program Tim is able to find humor almost everywhere. His outrageous stories and unusual props help audience members gain a fresh perspective on work and life through the principles of laughter. His props are fun and funny, but more importantly they reinforce his message of how to act and not just react to life's inconveniences. His stories hammer home his mantra of "first have fun for you, then develop it and use it by sharing it with others." Discover how to harness humor to instantly reduce stress and renew spirits through the day. Perfect as an opening or closing keynote, general session or evening event.

LEADERSHIP:
THE TAO OF HUMOR: WORKSHOP (ONE HOUR TO ½ DAY)

Although most everyone will agree how very powerful humor can be at work, misused, humor can have an equally damaging effect. In this laughter filled class discover how humor can be your most useful tool in dealing with the challenges of an ever changing workplace. Learn what's appropriate and what's not and how to always make "the farce" be with you. This class draws on Tim's extensive County, State and Federal work experience and provides valuable insights that will improve your effectiveness as a leader.

JUGGLING STRESS:
LAUGHTER WORKS: TEAM DEVELOPMENT (ONE HOUR)

How abut a fun, interactive, laugh-out-loud, low–impact team development event? This popular one – hour class helps participants rediscover and sharpen basic team development skills. Perfect as a separate event or combined with any other Comic Visions ® program.

_____

TIM'S TOYS

Stress-buster toys as seen in his Seminars: Order your very own nose-flutes, office owls, big bucks, crown of power and much more including:

_____

BOOKS

The Comic Visions Coloring Book. $ 5.00
This real life coloring book provides you with cartoons of Tim's most famous stories ready for you or any of your staff to color and place on your file cabinet for immediate stress relief. A really fun way to remind yourself (and everyone else) to use your Comic Vision throughout the day. Feel free to color outside the lines.

Motivational Leaders: $ 14.95
Motivational leaders shares the unmatched talent of fifteen of the world's leading motivational leadership experts. Each author provides wonderful stories, anecdotes, examples and quotations along with practical, useable information guaranteed to inspire and inform. Motivational leaders share strategies and perspectives that will motivate you…and help you to motivate others.:

VIDEO AND AUDIO TAPES

Video tapes: Developing a Comic Vision $ 39.00
Audiotapes: Developing a Comic Vision $ 10.00

ARTICLES ABOUT HUMOR AND HUMAN SERVICES BY TIM GARD, CSP

Visit: http://www.timgard.com

FOR MORE INFORMATION about **Comic Visions**® programs, or any Tim's Toy's products, visit his website at **http://www.timgard.com** or call him at 1-800-865-9939, or write to him at **Comic Visions**®, 4150 Ireland Street, Denver, CO 80249

HUMOR RESOURCES

AD-GRAPHICS
"From coast to coast, border to border, we help professional speakers make more money."
Jim Weems
1-800-368-6196
www.adgraf.com

AMERICAN ASSOCIATION OF THERAPEUTIC HUMOR
Publishes a quarterly newsletter and offers networking opportunities.
4534 West Butler Drive
Glendale, AZ 85302, phone: 623-934-6068
Fax: 623-934-5902, office@aath.org
Web: www.aath.org

BOOK PUBLISHERS: MC NAUGHTON & GUNN
Lori Potter
Phone: 800-368-6196
Lorip@mcnaughton-gunn.com

CLOWNS OF AMERICA INTERNATIONAL
National Clown Organization,
The New Calliope. Clowns of America International, Inc.
P.O. Box 6468, Lee's Summit, MO 64064-6468

DOM RINALDO
Caricaturist | Magician | Ventriloquist
Phone: 702-242-0215
Email: doodles50@juno.com

THE HUMOR PROJECT
Research on Humor, quarterly journal.
Humor Project/Sagmore Institute,
110 Spring Street, Saratoga Springs, NY 12866

HUMOR RESOURCES

ISHS
INTERNATIONAL SOCIETY OF HUMOR STUDIES
For more information, contact: Dr. Willibald Ruch
wruch@uni-duesseldorf.de

JAMES MALIA
Caricaturist
1231 Franciscan Court #6
Carpinteria, CA 93013
805-684-3124

JEST FOR THE HEALTH OF IT
Workshops for health care professional, authors,
presenters, and clowns. Patty Wooten, P.O. Box 8484,
Santa Cruz, CA 95061, Phone: 831-460-1600
Fax: 831-460-1601, PWooten@jesthealth.com

PANCAKE PRODUCTIONS
Simply silly hats.
Phone: 603-393-7714; FunE98@aol.com

SCOTT FRIEDMAN
"...Touching Hearts, Minds and Funny Bones"
Phone: (303) 671-7222 Fax (303) 368-5781
Email: scott@funnyscott.com
Web: www.funnyscott.com

SHANNON PARISH
COMPLETED PEOPLE®
"Illustrating Your Expertise!" | Cartoonist, Humorous Illustrator
Phone: 303-460-0605: Fax: 303-404-9487
Email: Shannon@completedpeople.com
Web: www.creativevirtualoffice.com | www.artbyshannon.com

HUMOR RESOURCES

STEVE KISSELL, CSP
Motivational humorist and national speaker providing keynotes,
seminars, and workshops on humor in the workplace and personal life.
1227 Manchester Avenue, Norfolk, VA 23508-1122
Phone: 757.423.3867; fax: 757.489.1587
KissellTalks@cs.com
Web: www.kisselltalks.com

THE STICKER MAN
Appreciation and custom-made stickers.
P. O. Box 5153, Jackson Beach, FL 32240
Phone: 904-223-5828; www.StickersRus.com

TIM GARD, CSP
COMIC VISION®
Phone: 800-865-9939: Fax: 303-932-0900
comicvisns@aol.com
Web: www.timgard.com

WHIM, WORLD HUMOR AND IRONY MEMBERSHIP
Annual interdisciplinary humor conference.
Don Nilsen, Ph.D., English Department,
Arizona State University, Tempe, AZ 85287

"WING TIPS"
A Great Travel Book by Allen Klein.
allenklein@aol.com